AF572238

2500 copies of this First Edition were
Printed in the Stonetone Process by
Rapoport Printing Corp., New York City,
United States of America

International Standard Book Number 0-915998-01-7

Two Hundred Years at the Old North Bridge

April 19, 1775

Paul Revere never made it to Concord. He was stopped by British officers outside Lexington, forced to dismount and to give up his horse. Fortunately, Revere had just met up with Samuel Prescott, on his way home to Concord after calling on his lady friend in Lexington, and told him the news of the British detachment marching out from Boston. Prescott escaped from the officers by spurring his horse over a stone wall, and completed the job of warning the residents of Concord.

When he heard Prescott's report, Colonel James Barrett, commander of the Concord militia, immediately started rounding up men, and sent riders out to nearby communities to summon other companies of Minutemen. By the time dawn was approaching, some 250 Minutemen had assembled at Concord. The town saddler, Reuben Brown, volunteered to ride to Lexington for news. He arrived just in time to hear the gunfire and see the rows of Redcoats through the smoke.

When Brown reported back what he had seen, the Concord militia formed into companies and started marching down the road toward Lexington, fife and drums in the lead. Then they spotted the well-disciplined red and white lines moving down the road toward them, sunlight glistening from bayonets and buckles. The militia did an about-face, marched quickly back to Concord, crossed the North Bridge, and took up positions on the high ground beyond. By now they had learned about the eight Minutemen who had been killed on the Lexington green. As the Minutemen watched, heavy smoke started curling up from a bonfire in town, and the colonials erroneously concluded that the British soldiers were burning their homes. The militia re-formed and marched back down toward the bridge.

Out front was Captain Isaac Davis, a gunsmith, commanding the Minutemen company from Acton. Three companies of Redcoats were stationed at the east end of the bridge, and at the approach of the militia they opened fire. Davis and another Acton man fell dead.

Then, for the first time in American history, citizens turned their guns on British troops. As the minutemen emptied their muskets, a dozen Redcoats fell to the ground — three of them dead, the others wounded. The remaining Redcoats took to their heels and ran off toward Concord.

Colonel Barrett and his men moved forward and deployed themselves behind stone walls. Other Minutemen streamed toward the area as news of Lexington and Concord spread through the surrounding countryside. After a long period of indecision, the British troops were ordered into line and headed out of town back toward Boston. All along the route they were subjected to cruel cross-fire from Yankee farmers and craftsmen concealed behind trees and rocks. British reinforcements at Lexington prevented more serious casualties, but by the time the detachment reached Boston Harbor late in the day, seventy-two Redcoats had been killed. The American Revolution had begun.

April 19, 1875

The high point of the nation's first Centennial celebration at Concord was the unveiling of the Statue of the Minuteman at the west end of the Old North Bridge. The event was a tribute to Yankee obstinacy and New England competitiveness.

Not long after the establishment of the new Republic, the forces of progress had caused the abandonment of the original North Bridge. The western end of the bridge was on low ground and was subject to flooding at high water. In 1793 the town fathers had moved the road to a higher point several hundred yards downstream, and built a new bridge.

When the town celebrated its own bicentennial in 1836, it constructed a monument in tribute to the Battle of 1775, but located the monument at the eastern end of the site of the old bridge. Ralph Waldo Emerson's "Concord Hymn" was sung at the ceremony marking the completion of the monument on July 4, 1837.

All of this did not seem quite right to Ebenezer Hubbard, a stubborn old farmer who lived alone in the house where his grandfather had entertained John Hancock and other members of the Continental Congress. He resented the fact that the battle monument had been erected at the *British* end of the bridge. So he decided to do something about it.

Farmer Hubbard presented the sum of $600 to the Town Treasurer as a contribution toward reconstructing the Old North Bridge. The town accepted the gift but did nothing to carry out its purposes.

Upon his death (at the age of 87) Hubbard's will revealed a more ingenious approach to the problem. He bequeathed the additional sum of $1000 to the town for the purpose of erecting a suitable monument on the American side of the bridge, and directed that if the town had not taken affirmative action on the monument within five years, then his executor was to give the money to the town of Hancock, New Hampshire, instead. That was in 1870.

The town of Concord duly appointed a committee to consider the matter. Then another factor entered the scene — the committee learned that the town officials of Lexington were considering plans for a bang-up Centennial Celebration in 1875 and had already commissioned two Italian sculptors to carve marble statues of John Hancock and Samuel Adams (who had been hiding out in Lexington at the time of the battle in 1775) to be installed in Lexington's Memorial Hall. The Concord committee duly recommended to the Town Meeting in March, 1873 the erection of a statue at the western edge of the former bridge, as well as the reconstruction of the bridge itself. The idea for the monument's design was a statue of a Minuteman.

Because of the shortage of funds, the Concord officials could not afford to commission an established European sculptor, and instead had to settle for a promising but completely unknown youngster from town, named French. A modest sum was appropriated to fill in the ground at the bridge site to avoid flooding, and arrangements were made to have a base cut from the very same granite boulder from which the earlier battle monument had been created. The base was duly installed at a point just in front of the stump of the apple tree where Isaac Davis reportedly fell, and inscribed with the first verse of Emerson's "Concord Hymn."

Meanwhile, the town of Concord had respectfully declined an invitation from the town officials of Lexington to plan a joint centennial celebration, and instead decided to go it alone. The competition between the two towns' Centennial Committees grew to fever pitch as April, 1875 approached. The tension was compounded by the failure of Lexington's marble statues to arrive from Italy. The statues were shipped separately — one on a steamer which was not scheduled to dock until a day-and-a-half before the celebration; the other on a brig reported weather-bound at Martha's Vineyard. A Coast Guard cutter took the brig in tow and brought her into Boston. Teams of horses rushed both statues to Lexington, where they were installed just twelve hours before their dedication was scheduled to begin.

Meanwhile, at Concord, the river was in flood stage and the knoll with the new Minuteman statue was cut off by high water from the main celebration area which was to be on the site where the militia had organized for the assault against the British. Nature was provident, however, the flood receded just in time to permit the ceremony to go ahead as planned.

April 19, 1875, was bitterly cold. Two giant tents were set up in the meadow on the west side of the Old North Bridge, which had itself been reconstructed in "rustic style", complete with benches for resting. The "oration tent" boasted a wooden platform with 200 seats for dignitaries. An audience of an estimated 6000 was expected to stand. The "dinner tent" was larger and elegantly decked out with bunting, flags and streamers.

The great day began with a cannon salute of one hundred rounds at dawn. The temperature was 22 degrees. The first train from Boston arrived at 7:30 a.m. The official reception committee sublimely greeted the first arrivals, confident of their months of careful planning to handle an estimated crowd of 20,000. Soon other trains arrived. Then more after them. The crowd swelled to 50,000 and the committee abandoned all hope of maintaining order. The town was overrun. Food gave out. The saloons were closed down by the officials, creating a field day for enterprising bootleggers who had foreseen the possibility and were prepared for a brisk business. Fortunately the trains were also able to carry people away, and after the tens of thousands who found they could not get inside the official tents tired of wandering about, they began to leave.

Things were not so fortunate in Lexington, where the hungry mobs rushed the official dinner tent before the invited guests were seated, and scooped up most of the food. When those with tickets finally made their way to their places the tent was in shambles. No one felt much like eating. The Boston Evening Transcript reported, "The only thing that was warm at the centennial dinner in Lexington was the ice cream."

In Concord the official parade got under way at 10:00 a.m., marching down Main Street, past Monument Square, across the Old North Bridge and up to the tents. Near the head of the procession rode the President of the United States, Ulysses S. Grant, in a barouche drawn by four bay horses and accompanied by the Vice-President, Secretary of State, and his military aide. The crowd applauded politely.

When the President's party reached the site of the Minuteman statue, the chairman of the Monument Committee stepped forward and pulled a cord to remove the covering. The crowd cheered. Then the President moved into the oration tent where he joined other dignitaries on the platform. The crowd filed in to maximum capacity, and the speaking began. It was destined to continue for almost six hours.

The master of ceremonies was Ebenezer Rockwood Hoar, of Concord, a warm and charming man who held everyone's attention. The parade of speakers included Ralph Waldo Emerson, then 72, and James Russell Lowell. President Grant was not invited to speak. At ten minutes of one, the proceedings were suspended briefly while the President and his Cabinet departed to spend the second half of the day at Lexington.

Meanwhile the carpenters who had built the

platform for the dignitaries apparently had miscalculated, for twice during the day the platform collapsed with a thunderous roar. The first collapse occurred while the President was on the platform, causing one wag to shout out, "That evidently is not a third-term platform." The President did not smile.

April 19, 1975

Having learned their lesson a hundred years before, the planning committee for Concord's next Centennial Celebration were determined to keep rigid control on the size of the crowd. Everything was planned with care. The woods would be cordoned off to reduce automobile traffic. The celebration would be kept low-key with just the traditional reenactment of Paul Revere's ride and the walk of local residents from Acton to Concord. One special touch: the importation of a troop of Redcoats from England for the reenactment of the incident on Lexington Green. All was carefully laid out.

Then things began to go wrong. The President of the United States, Gerald R. Ford, announced his intention to go to Concord and Lexington for the festivities.

Then, a few days before the celebration, a group of long-haired youths calling themselves the "People's Bicentennial Commission," committed to end "corporate tyranny," applied for a camping permit from the National Park Service to use the knoll near the Old North Bridge. A nervous Federal administrator granted the permit, to the consternation of local residents.

Once again the crowds descended on Concord and Lexington — an estimated 200,000 in all. When the police closed off the roads, the procession kept moving in on bicycles, on foot and even in canoes. The campers were greeted by chilly rainfall and soon ran out of beer. Folksingers Pete Seeger and Arlo Guthrie entertained the crowded campground.

When the President arrived on the morning of April 19, he found himself confronted by a crowd of youthful hecklers. He stiffly placed a wreath at the base of Daniel Chester French's now world-famous statue. Then, amid catcalls and jeers, he raced through a speech on America's military might. With a look of relief he ducked away from the twentieth-century protestors at Concord and made his way to a more friendly reception at Lexington.

Despite the stiff formal proceedings and the planning mishaps, however, the Bicentennial Celebration at Concord was a memorable event for tens of thousands who participated in it.

The sensitive and perceptive photographs by Gabriel Seymour in this small volume show glimpses of the Americans who came in large numbers to worship at one of the shrines of their liberty — boy scouts, girl scouts, high school students, mothers and fathers, history buffs, soldiers, local residents. For them, the celebration at the Old North Bridge on April 19 was an event to be remembered.

Bicentennial Addresses by President Gerald R. Ford

Boston, Massachusetts

The President's Remarks at the Old North Church Bicentennial Lantern Service. April 18, 1975

Two hundred years ago tonight, two lanterns hung in the belfry of this Old North Church. Those lanterns signaled patriots on the other side of the Charles River British troops were moving by water. As Longfellow said in his poem: "One if by land, and two if by sea."

Paul Revere, William Dawes, Samuel Prescott rode into the night, alerting the colonists the British were coming. When day broke, according to the diaries of the time, the sky was clear and blue.

British troops had crossed the Charles River. They marched all night, and after a skirmish at Lexington, the Redcoats arrived at Concord. There a volley was fired by our Minutemen, what Emerson called "the shot heard 'round the world." The American war for independence had begun.

Tonight, we stand in tribute to those who stood for liberty and for us, two centuries ago. Tonight, we bow our heads in memory of those who gave their lives, their limbs, their property for us during that historic struggle, because tonight we begin as a Nation and as a people the celebration of our Bicentennial.

Alexis de Tocqueville, the French historian, wrote of our beginnings: "In that land, the great experiment was to be made, by civilized men, of the attempt to construct society on a new basis."

Over the decades, there were challenges to that experiment. Could a nation half slave and half free survive? Could a society with such a mixture of peoples and races and religions succeed? Would the new Nation be swallowed up in the materialism of its own well-being? The answers are found in the history of our land and our people.

It is said that a national character is shaped by the interplay of inheritance, environment, and historical experience. Our inheritance is basically that of Western Europe. From the English, we received the traditions of liberty, laws, language, and customs.

The American inheritance has been constantly enriched by people from Western and Eastern Europe, from Asia and Africa, as well as Latin America and many other parts of this great globe. Over 200 years, some 50 million immigrants have been absorbed in our society. Though our national origins are not forgotten, all of us are proud to be simply called Americans.

Our environment includes every variety of climate, soil, and resources. The American historical experience has been brief compared to many, many other nations. We are the new world, but we are the world's oldest republic.

The most distinguished characteristic of our American way is our individualism. It is reflected in our frontier spirit, our private enterprise, and our ability to organize and to produce. Our ability to adopt new ideas and to adapt them to practical purposes is also strikingly American.

But now we ask ourselves, how did we come to be where we are tonight? The answer is found in the history of the American experience. It teaches us that the American experience has been more of reason than revolution, more of principles than passions, and more of hope than hostility or despair.

But our history is also one of paradox. It has shown us that reason is not without its moments of rebellion, that principles are not without passion, and hope is not without its hours of discouragement and dismay.

It is well to recall this evening that America was born of both promise and protest—the promise of religious and civil liberties, and protest for representation and against repression.

Some of our dreams have at times turned to disappointment and disillusionment, but adversity has also driven Americans to greater heights. George Washington marched from the anguish of Valley Forge to the acclaim of final victory.

Reason and hope were the twin lanterns of Washington's life. They enabled him to prevail over the day-to-day doubts and defeats. They have been the lamps that have lighted the road of America toward its ultimate goals—dignity, and self-fulfillment—and yes, pride in country.

Abraham Lincoln was a man of reason and a man of hope. He acknowledged the grave flaw of our first 87 years—slavery.

Over 110 years ago, the American Civil War ended with our Republic battered and divided. Many people talked more of survival than of union. One-half of the Nation was on its knees in ruin. Nearly 2 million had been killed and wounded. The war had uprooted the lives and fortunes of millions more. Its end was marked by more tears than cheers, but it was also the birth of a new Nation freeing itself from human slavery.

Just before the war ended, on March 4, 1865, President Abraham Lincoln stood on the East Portico of the Capitol in Washington and delivered his second inaugural address. He extended the hand of friendship and unity when he said, "With malice toward none, with charity for all, with firmness in the right, as God gives us to see the right, let us strive on to finish the work we are in, to bind up the Nation's wounds."

President Lincoln had relit the lamps of reason and the lamps of hope. He had rekindled pride in America.

Over 100 years ago, as the Nation celebrated its centennial, America looked to the future. Our Nation had emerged from an agricultural, frontier society into the industrial age. Our towns were beginning to evolve into the cities of the 20th century. Rail transportation and telegraph were tying this vast continent together. When we celebrated our 100th birthday, one of the themes was: "While proud of what we have done, we regret that we have not done more."

There was certainly more to do and more people to do the job. Immigrants were pouring into America. They were welcomed by these words inscribed on the Statue of Liberty: "I lift my lamp beside the golden door." The great increase in the number of Americans, made us a formidable force in the world. That force was soon needed. World War I saw American troops fight and die in Europe for the first time.

Many Americans were disappointed and disillusioned by the aftermath of the war. They found the causes for which they fought unachieved. The American people rejected foreign entanglements and withdrew into a separate existence. They wanted to be left alone.

In 1941, the United States was attacked, and once more we went to war—this time across the Pacific as well as the Atlantic. We were proud of this country and what it was achieving for liberty around the world.

Yet, still another time, following victory over our enemies, the American public was jarred and disillusioned by the postwar years. They discovered there would be no real peace. Europe was divided in two on V–E Day. In the words of Churchill, "An iron curtain has descended across the continent." America had become the stronghold of liberty.

President Truman instituted a bipartisan foreign policy of containment, cooperation, and reconstruction. The Marshall Plan moved to reconstruct the free world; the United Nations was born. But the cold war had already begun. Soon, all too soon, America was again at war under the banner of the United Nations in Korea.

Little did we know then that American troops would only a decade later be fighting still another war in Asia, culminating in a broken peace agreement in Vietnam.

In the 200 years of our existence, it is not war and disillusionment which have triumphed. No; it is the American concept and fulfillment of liberty that have truly revolutionized the world. America has not sought the conquest of territory but instead, the mutual support of all men and women who cherish freedom.

The Declaration of Independence has won the minds,

it has won the hearts of this world beyond the dreams of any revolutionary who has ever lived. The two lanterns of Old North Church have fired a torch of freedom that has been carried to the ends of the world.

As we launch this Bicentennial celebration, we Americans must remind ourselves of the eternal truths by which we live. We must be reinspired by the great ideals that created our country. We must renew ourselves as a people and rededicate this Nation to the principles of two centuries ago.

We must revitalize the pride in America that has carried us from some of our darkest hours to our brightest days. We must once again become masters of our own destiny. This calls for patience, for understanding, for tolerance, and work toward unity—unity of purpose, a unity based on reason, a unity based on hope.

This call is not new. It is as old as the Continental Congress of 200 years ago, as legendary as Lincoln's legacy of more than 100 years ago, and as relevant as today's call to Americans to join in the celebration of the Bicentennial.

Perhaps national unity is an impossible dream. Like permanent peace, perhaps it will prove to be a never-ending search. But today we celebrate the most impossible dream of our history, the survival of the Government and the permanence of our principles of our Founding Fathers.

America and its principles have not only survived but flourished far beyond anyone's dreams. No nation in history has undertaken the enormous enterprises of the American people. No country, despite our imperfections, has done more to bring economic and social justice to its people and to the world.

Yet, we have suffered great internal turmoil and torment in recent years. Nevertheless, in all of the explosive changes of this and past generations, the American people have demonstrated a rich reserve of reason and of hope.

There are few times in our history when the American people have spoken with more eloquent reason and hope than during the tribulations and tests that our Government and our economic system have endured during the past year. Yet, the American people have stood firm.

The Nation has not been torn with irresponsible reaction. Rather, we are blessed with patience, common sense, and a willingness to work things out. The American dream is not dead. It simply has yet to be fulfilled.

In the economy and energy and the environment, in housing, in transportation, in education and communication, in social problems and social planning, America has yet to realize its greatest contribution to civilization.

To do this, America needs new ideas and new efforts from our people. Each of us, of every color, of every creed, are part of our country and must be willing to build not only a new and better Nation but new and greater understanding and unity among our people.

Let us not only be a Nation of peace but let us foster peace among all nations. Let us not only believe in equality but live it each day in our lives. Let us not only feed and clothe a healthy America but let us lend a hand to others struggling for self-fulfillment. Let us seek even greater knowledge and offer the enlightenment of our endeavors to the educational and scientific community throughout the world. Let us seek the spiritual enrichment of our people more than material gains. Let us be true to ourselves, to our heritage, and to our homeland, and we will never then be false to any people or to any nation.

Finally, let us pray here in the Old North Church tonight that those who follow 100 years or 200 years from now may look back at us and say: We were a society which combined reason with liberty and hope with freedom.

May it be said above all: We kept the faith. Freedom flourished. Liberty lived. These are the abiding principles of our past and the greatest promise of our future.

Following the President's remarks, two lanterns were lighted by Robert Newman Ruggles and Robert Newman Sheet, descendants of Robert Newman, who, as sexton of the Old North Church in 1775, lighted the two lanterns which signaled the movement of British troops. The President then lighted a third lantern which marked the beginning of America's third century.

Concord, Massachusetts

The President's Remarks at Patriots Day Ceremonies at the Old North Bridge. April 19, 1975

Two hundred years ago today, American Minutemen raised their muskets at the Old North Bridge and answered a British volley. Ralph Waldo Emerson called it "the shot heard 'round the world." The British were in full retreat soon afterwards and returned to Boston. But there was no turning back for the colonists—the American Revolution had begun.

Today, two centuries later, the President of 50 united States and 213 million people stands before a new generation of Americans who have come to this hallowed ground.

In these two centuries, the United States has become a world power. From a newborn Nation with a few ships, American seapower now ranges to the most distant shores. From a militia of raw recruits, the American military stands on the frontlines of the free world. Our fliers and our planes eclipse one another in power and in speed with each suceeding new breed of airmen and aircraft.

From a Nation virtually alone, America is now allied with many free worlds [nations] in common defense. The concepts of isolationism and fortress America no longer represent either the reasoning or the role of the United States foreign policy.

World leadership was thrust upon America, and we have assumed it. In accepting that role, the United States has assumed responsibility from which it cannot and will not retreat. Free nations need the United States, and we need free nations. Neither can go it alone.

There are some in the world who still believe that force and the threat of force are the major instruments of national and international policy. They believe that military supremacy over others is [the] logical and legitimate [end] of their revolutionary doctrines. Such aims have left a trail of tyranny, broken promises, and falsehood.

Tyranny by any other name is still tyranny. Broken promises in any other language are still promises unkept. And falsehood by any other description is still a lie.

This is not the rhetoric of the past. It is reason about the present because history keeps repeating itself. Force as an instrument of national and international policy continues to be a major instrument of change in the world. Reasonable societies and reasonable people must do all in their power to reconcile all threats to peace. Now is a time for reconciliation, not recrimination. It is a time of reconstruction, not rancor.

The world is witnessing revolutionary technological, economic, and social change—a massive and rapid breaking of barriers.

We, all men and women of all lands, must master this change. We must make this revolution an evolution—to make and accept change with greater order and greater restraint.

How can we achieve, how can we accomplish this evolution? It is not enough to call upon material resources. No material resources are sufficient to themselves to inspire the continued confidence of men in reasonable change. We must summon higher, greater values as we proceed. These higher values are found in the principles of this Republic, forged by our forefathers in the Declaration of Independence.

Thomas Jefferson wrote of change in the light of American principles, and he said, "Nothing, then, is unchangeable but the inherent and inalienable rights of man." Jefferson accepted change in the ordinary course of human events, but he rejected any fundamental change in the principles of our Republic, the inalienable rights of man.

Often, change is healthy for a people and a nation. That is why America has always been a land of new horizons and new hopes. Free choice, the consent of the governed, represents the American philosophy of change.

Life, liberty, and the pursuit of happiness are sacred rights, not to be given or not to be taken by shifting winds or changing moods. It is important to recall these truths because the men and women of America must renew that faith, their courage, and their confidence. Our belief, our commitment to human rights, to human liberties, must also represent belief and commitment to ourselves.

It is a time to place the hand of healing on the heart of America—not division and not blame. When all is said and done, the finest tribute that may ever be paid this Nation and this people is that we provided a home for freedom.

Freedom was nourished in American soil because the principles of the Declaration of Independence flourished in our land. These principles, when enunciated 200 years ago, were a dream, not a reality. Today, they are real. Equality has matured in America. Our inalienable rights have become even more sacred. There is no government in our land without the consent of the governed.

Many other lands have freely accepted the principles of liberty and freedom in the Declaration of Independence and fashioned their own independent republics. It is these principles, freely taken and freely shared, that have revolutionized the world. The volley fired here at Concord two centuries ago, "the shot heard 'round the world," still echoes today on this anniversary.

One hundred years from now, a new generation of Americans will come here to rededicate this Nation and renew the spirit of our people in the principles that inspire us on this occasion. Let it be said that those of us who came to Concord today reaffirmed these final words of the Declaration of Independence: "We mutually pledge to each other our lives, our fortunes and our sacred honor."

Following the President's remarks, Sir Peter Ramsbotham, British Ambassador to the United States, laid a wreath on the graves of the British soldiers. The President then placed a wreath at the base of the Minutemen Statue.

Concord Hymn

by

RALPH WALDO EMERSON

By the rude bridge that arched the flood,
   Their flag to April's breeze unfurled,
Here once the embattled farmers stood
   And fired the shot heard round the world.

The foe long since in silence slept;
   Alike the conquerer silent sleeps;
And Time the ruined bridge has swept
   Down the dark stream which seaward creeps.

On this green bank, by this soft stream,
   We set to-day a votive stone;
That memory may their deed redeem,
   When, like our sires, our sons are gone.

Spirit, that made those heroes dare
   To die, and leave their children free,
Bid Time and Nature gently spare
   The shaft we raise to them and thee.

SUNG AT THE COMPLETION OF THE BATTLE MONUMENT, JULY 4, 1837

NO PARKING
Concord
1775-1975

LINE OF MARCH
APRIL 19, 1775

DISC
CLIN
THICKLY SETTLED
BOY SCOUT TROOP 156
OF
PEACE LUTHERAN CHURCH
DISCO UTICA MICH.

DERBY
DISTRICT 2
OCEAN COUNTY COUNCIL

Penn Hills

3rd Regt.
N. Jersey

BEDFORD
1774
MINUTEMEN

MANILA 1899
MEXICO
GETTYSBURG
UNITED

106mm
187 BG
3 18 1
CS
57

GRAVE OF BRITISH SOLDIERS
CAME THREE THOUSAND MILES AND
TO KEEP THE
ON ITS THRONE:
UNHEARD. BEYOND THE OCEAN
MOTHER MADE HER MOAN
APRIL 19, 1775
IN MEMORY